Praise for Al

"I have come to know that sometimes the simplest words can make a major difference in how people perceive and interact with their world. This book can make that same difference to you."

—Jack Canfield,
coauthor of *Chicken Soup for the Soul*

"Allen Klein is a noble and vital force watching over the human condition."

—Jerry Lewis,
actor/comedian

"I am always looking for ideas that help people enrich their lives. This book does just that. I highly recommend you read it...it will feed your soul, lift your spirits, and help you live a fuller, richer, and more joy-filled life."

—SARK (Susan Ariel Rainbow Kennedy),
author of *Living Juicy*

"Allen Klein's purpose is to make us feel inspired again, to bask in laughter and revel in joy."

—*OMTimes*

"Allen's collection is a great place to find some never-before-seen quotes that will make your communication more intriguing. Read it and reap."

—Sam Horn,
author of *POP!: Create the Perfect Pitch, Title, and Tagline for Anything*

"Words to live by are just words, unless you actually live by them. Take these words and love them—take these words and LIVE them!"

—BJ Gallagher,
author of *It's Never Too Late to Be What You Might Have Been*

"Let Allen inspire you and help you embrace and celebrate the joy in your life and in the life that surrounds you."

—Carole Brody Fleet,
author of *Happily Even After*

"As marketable as the text is for gift-giving, it's also a great idea to keep your own copy for lonely times. Flipping through it at the beginning or end of each day can give you a little boost."

—Psych Central

"This book will wake you up and show you how this day may truly be the best day of your life."

—Kristine Carlson,
coauthor of the *Don't Sweat the Small Stuff* series

"This powerful collection of quotes serves as a great reminder of simple truths and timeless wisdom that can alter our lives in a profound way. This book is guaranteed to inspire all who read it."

—Mike Robbins,
author of *Focus on the Good Stuff*

Positive Thoughts for Troubling Times

Also by Allen Klein:

Positive Thoughts for Troubling Times

A Renew-Your-Spirit Guide

Allen Klein

Best-selling author of
The Healing Power of Humor

Foreword by Heidi Hanna, PhD
Author of *Stressaholic* and executive director
of the American Institute of Stress

Mango Publishing
CORAL GABLES

Cover Design: Roberto Núñez
Layout & Design: Roberto Núñez

For permission requests, please contact the publisher at:
Mango Publishing Group
2850 S Douglas Road, 2nd Floor
Coral Gables, FL 33134 USA
info@mango.bz

For special orders, quantity sales, course adoptions and corporate sales, please email the publisher at sales@mango.bz. For trade and wholesale sales, please contact Ingram Publisher Services at customer.service@ingramcontent.com or +1.800.509.4887.

Positive Thoughts for Troubling Times: A Renew-Your-Spirit Guide

Library of Congress Cataloging-in-Publication number: 2019932089
ISBN: (print) 978-1-63353-956-3, (ebook) 978-1-63353-957-0
BISAC category code: REF019000 REFERENCE / Quotations

Printed in the United States of America

For all those who are peacemakers in the world,
All those who work to right wrongs,
And those who are going through their own troubling times.

"Positive thinking is powerful thinking. If you want happiness, fulfillment, success, and inner peace, start thinking you have the power to achieve those things. Focus on the bright side of life and expect positive results."

—Germany Kent

Table of Contents

Foreword

When Allen asked if I would be willing to share some words to introduce his next literary creation, I jumped at the chance to contribute. In fact, I started writing the foreword by going on and on about how inspiring and entertaining Allen's words were, and how he was once again revolutionizing the way we look at the world. That was long before I realized it was mainly a collection of quotes from other people. Then, with a massive smile and an internal giggle, I realized that he had once again found a new way to sneak some serious delight into my day.

Positive Thoughts for Troubling Times is special and needed, considering the fact that the words we use and the thoughts we think literally shape our experience of the world. As a stress expert, and as someone who's pretty good at stressing myself, I've seen firsthand the damage done by the wrong kind of inner dialogue.

Despite more knowledge about stress—both its causes and its comforts—we've never been more in need of a cure. Research suggests that 75-90 percent of medical visits are stress-related. We are tired and wired and in need of a new direction—which is where *Positive Thoughts for Troubling Times* comes in.

Fortunately for us all, Allen Klein has stepped up to serve as a guide to organize important wisdom from some of our most transformational leaders in a way that is both entertaining and energizing. The thoughts, reflections, insights, and new directions provided in this inspiring book serve as an internal GPS for our souls as we navigate the stress of our daily lives.

I invite you to join me in using the positive thoughts shared in this book as a mantra of sorts. They can comfort you in times of confusion and challenge. They can provide course corrections when you require a change of pace. Perhaps most important of all, follow Allen's guidance in these pages as he provides you with the structure to look into the seemingly simple choices we make and become curious about more positive directions—and to grow stronger and more resilient as a result.

Heidi Hanna, PhD
Author of *Stressaholic* and executive director
of the American Institute of Stress

Introduction

One of the first shows I saw on Broadway was *Carousel*. I was seven years old at the time. Shortly after, a favorite uncle of mine died. A song from the show helped me deal with my loss. The lyrics spoke about holding your head up high when you go through a storm and not being afraid of the dark. It also reminded me that at the end of the storm, there is always a golden sky.

Those words, and numerous inspirational others, comforted me not only at that time, but in many of the dark times I experienced during the years that followed.

The right words at just the right time can be powerful companions to lift you up when the world is bringing you down. Carefully chosen thoughts can be a guide to help you maneuver trying times. They can be an inspiration to help you rise above any situation.

It is my hope that the thoughts in this book bring you comfort and perhaps ease the pain of your troubling moments.

You can read the book in sequential order, if you choose. But my favorite way to read a book of this type is to think about what difficulty I am experiencing and then randomly open to any page and see what advice it presents. See what calls out to you and embrace those words. If nothing sings to you, continue searching until something does.

In any case, it is not really important how you read this book. What is more important is that you read it, read it again, and perhaps even post a quotation or two where you can see it on a regular basis.

And, remember…words are powerful. May those in this book enrich and empower your life.

Allen Klein
San Francisco, CA
www.allenklein.com

A Matter of Choice

We are the choices we make. Each and every second of the day we are making decisions. Some of them are major…should we get married, raise a family, move to a new city? Others are more mundane…which video to view, restaurant to patronize, emails to answer?

Even a stop at a Starbucks for a simple cup of coffee is not so simple. Do you want regular or decaf, black, regular milk, soy milk, or almond milk, espresso Americano or espresso latte, or something special like a Salted Caramel Mocha Frappuccino®? Or on the other hand, should you just chuck the whole coffee experience and maybe order a steamed apple juice or hot chocolate instead?

The point is that one cup of coffee might not make much difference in your life. But so many other decisions do. We therefore need to choose wisely. Hopefully the thoughts in this section will help you do just that.

When it rains, it pours. Maybe the art of life is to convert
tough times to great experiences:
we can choose to hate the rain or dance in it.

—Joan Marques

Everything can be taken from a man but one thing:
the last of the human freedoms—to choose one's attitude in
any given set of circumstances, to choose one's own way.

—Victor Frankl

The meaning of things lies not in the things
themselves but in our attitude towards them.

—Antoine de Saint-Exupéry

You always have two choices with your life and
experience: you can either learn from it or you
can place blame. The choice is always yours.

—Kevin Horsley

No one forces a person to be negative, and no one forces anyone to be positive. The choice is up to an individual and that person alone.

—Byron Pulsifer

That's the nice thing about being human. We only have one life, but we can choose what kind of story it's going to be.

—Rick Riordan

We are the choices we make.

—Patrick Ness

You have a choice, you either give it your best, or alternatively, you give up. Don't look back upon your life with regret, make the changes you want and make them now!

—Darren Housley

Every day, you make choices about what you will dedicate your time to, how you will spend your money, and who you will rely on. In every aspect of your life, you have the ability to choose either simplicity or complexity; finances, work, chores, shopping, entertainment, and relationships may all be sources of stress and chaos, or they may become wellsprings of peace and contentment.

—Chelsea Walters

The choice we make will determine whether we reinforce a world where conflicts escalate out of control, or create a new world where conflicts are transformed into opportunity.

—Mark Gerzon

I keep the telephone of my mind open to peace, harmony, health, love, and abundance. Then, whenever doubts, anxiety, or fear try to call me, they keep getting a busy signal—and soon they'll forget my number.

—Edith Armstrong

There is always plenty to be worried and sad
about, but there is equally plenty to be happy
and at peace with. The choice is yours.

—Steve Maraboli

No matter what's happening, choose to be happy.

—Joel Osteen

The greatest part of our happiness or misery depends
on our dispositions and not on our circumstances.

—Martha Washington

Happiness is an attitude. We either make ourselves miserable,
or happy and strong. The amount of work is the same.

—Francesca Reigler

A happy person is not a person in a certain
set of circumstances, but rather a person
with a certain set of attitudes.

—Hugh Downs

In every crisis, doubt, or confusion, take the higher path—
the path of compassion, courage, understanding, and love.

—Amit Ray

Sometimes, there is a lot of darkness in this world.
As I see it, you have two choices. You can be a part of
that darkness or you can be the light. Be the light.

—Tom Giaquinto

I think when tragedy occurs, it presents a choice. You
can give in to the void: the emptiness that fills your
heart, your lungs, that constricts your ability to think
or even breathe. Or you can try to find meaning.

—Sheryl Sandberg

You've got a lot of choices. If getting out of bed
in the morning is a chore and you're not smiling
on a regular basis, try another choice.

—Steven D. Woodhull

If you don't like where you are, move. You're not a tree.

—Peter Shankman

You have the choice this very moment—the only moment
you have for certain. I hope you aren't so wrapped up
in nonessential stuff that you forget to really enjoy
yourself—because this moment is about to be over.

—Oprah Winfrey

Every day we have plenty of opportunities to get
angry, stressed, or offended. But what you're doing
when you indulge these negative emotions is giving
something outside yourself power over your happiness.
You can choose to not let little things upset you.

—Joel Osteen

If you ever find yourself in the wrong story, leave.

—Mo Willems

If you don't like something change it; if you can't
change it, change the way you think about it.

—Mary Engelbreit

Even a thought, even a possibility can
shatter us and transform us.

—Friedrich Nietzsche

Destiny is not a matter of chance, it is a matter of choice;
it is not a thing to be waited for, it a thing to be achieved.

—William Jennings Bryan

Ultimately…it's not the stories that determine our
choices, but the stories that we continue to choose.

—Sylvia Boorstein

To be wronged is nothing unless you choose to remember it.

—Confucius

Your choice of people to associate with, both
personally and business-wise, is one of the most
important choices you make. If you associate with
turkeys, you will never fly with the eagles.

—Brian Tracy

Every person, all the events of your life are there
because you have drawn them there. What you
choose to do with them is up to you.

—Richard Bach

Look to your heart and soul first, rather than
looking to your head first, when choosing. Rather
than what you think, consider instead how you
feel. Look to the nature of things. Feel your choices
and decisions. It just might change everything.

—Jeffrey R. Anderson

When you make choices, please remember: what is good for you but not good for others won't be good for you either, eventually; what's good for you and others but not good for the Earth won't be good for you or others either, eventually; what's good for you, others, and the Earth will be good for all.

—Ilchi Lee

Believe in Yourself

When I was seven years old, my parents took me to see my first Broadway show. From that day on, I wanted to be a scenic designer, someone who created those pretty stage pictures.

In grade school, my fellow classmates would write book reports. I, on the other hand, made a book-related diorama in an old shoe box. In high school, I took myself downtown and saw almost every show on Broadway. In college, I designed many of the school productions, and, with the help of one of the professors, got into Yale Drama School.

It was a three-year master's degree program. They admitted twelve students the first year. Then, because they only produced eight plays in their smaller theater the second year, they let go of four designers. I was one of the first to go. In essence, they were telling me that I had no talent.

Soon after being booted from Yale, I became an apprentice in the scenic design union in New York City and finally became a full-fledged designer at CBS Television. My Yale classmates were still designing school productions. I was designing national television shows such as *Captain Kangaroo*, *The Merv Griffin Show*, and *The Jackie Gleason Show*.

Who said I had no talent? Who said I would never be a designer? Nobody could tell me I wasn't one. In my mind, I had been a scenic designer since I went to grade school. I believed in myself, my talents, and my dream.

Hopefully the following powerful thoughts will encourage you to believe in yourself too.

Greatness is not this wonderful, esoteric, elusive, god-like feature that only the special among us will ever taste, it's something that truly exists in all of us.

—Will Smith

I wish I could show you when you are lonely or in darkness the astonishing light of your own being.

—Hafez

There is a light which cannot ever be extinguished. It is inside of you. It is you.

—Neale Donald Walsch

Know yourself. Don't accept your dog's admiration as conclusive evidence that you are wonderful.

—Ann Landers

If you believe in yourself, anything is possible.

—Miley Cyrus

It is only in our darkest hours that we may discover
the true strength of the brilliant light within
ourselves that can never, ever, be dimmed.

—Doe Zantamata

We are all of us stars, and we deserve to twinkle.

—Marilyn Monroe

No one is perfect…absolutely no one. Like precious
stones, we have a few flaws, but why focus on
that? Focus on what you like about yourself, and
that will bring you happiness and peace.

—Richard Simmons

If we walk the victim, we're perceived as the victim.
And if we enter… glowing and receptive… if we
maintain our radiance and enter a situation with
radiance, often radiance will come our way.

—Patti Smith

I believe that God has put gifts and talents and ability on the inside of every one of us. When you develop that and you believe in yourself and you believe that you're a person of influence and a person of purpose, I believe you can rise up out of any situation.

—Joel Osteen

We don't even know how strong we are until we are forced to bring that hidden strength forward. In times of tragedy, of war, of necessity, people do amazing things. The human capacity for survival and renewal is awesome.

—Isabel Allende

Use what you've been through as fuel, believe in yourself, and be unstoppable!

—Yvonne Pierre

Our deepest fear is not that we are inadequate. Our deepest fear is that we are powerful beyond measure.

—Marianne Williamson

I find that when we really love and accept and approve of ourselves exactly as we are, then everything in life works.

—Louise Hay

Wouldn't it be powerful if you fell in love with yourself so deeply that you would do just about anything if you knew it would make you happy? This is precisely how much life loves you and wants you to nurture yourself. The deeper you love yourself, the more the universe will affirm your worth. Then you can enjoy a lifelong love affair that brings you the richest fulfillment from inside out.

—Alan Cohen

You yourself, as much as anyone in the entire universe, deserve your love and affection.

—The Buddha

Your relationship with yourself is the blueprint for all the relationships in your life. Want more love in your life? Be more loving toward yourself.

—Susyn Reeve

To love oneself is the beginning of a lifelong romance.

—Oscar Wilde

When one is out of touch with oneself,
one cannot touch others.

—Anne Morrow Lindbergh

Though we travel the world over to find the beautiful,
we must carry it with us or we find it not.

—Ralph Waldo Emerson

Everything is within your power,
and your power is within you.

—Janice Trachtman

Use what talents you possess; the woods would be very
silent if no birds sang except those that sang best.

—Henry van Dyke

We are each gifted in a unique and important way. It is our privilege and our adventure to discover our own special light.

—Mary Dunbar

Only when we are brave enough to explore the darkness will we discover the infinite power of our light.

—Brené Brown

Self-empowerment is free to anyone who chooses to use it. It comes from within and nowhere else. You cannot buy it, borrow it, steal it, or sell it. It is always available to you and never wears out. The only choice you have to make is whether or not you will use it.

—Gary Hopkins

Don't undermine your worth by comparing yourself with others. It is because we are different that each of us is special.

—Brian Dyson

Always be yourself and have faith in yourself. Do not go out and look for a successful personality and try to duplicate it.

—Bruce Lee

I never wanted to be the best.
I just wanted to be the best damn me.

—Lily Tomlin

Trust yourself. Create the kind of self that you will be happy to live with all your life. Make the most of yourself by fanning the tiny, inner sparks of possibility into flames of achievement.

—Golda Meir

Tough times never last, but tough people do.

—Robert H. Schuller

Because one believes in oneself, one doesn't try to convince others. Because one is content with oneself, one doesn't need others' approval. Because one accepts oneself, the whole world accepts him or her.

—Lao-Tzu

Often people attempt to live their lives backwards, they try to have more things or more money in order to do more of what they want so that they will be happier. The way it actually works is the reverse. You must first be who you really are, then do what you need to do in order to have what you want.

—Margaret Young

You are as amazing as you let yourself be. Let me repeat that. You are as amazing as you let yourself be.

—Elizabeth Alraune

Do something not because you think it might make money; do it because it makes your heart sing.

—Marianne Williamson

If you bring forth what is within you, what you bring forth
will save you. If you do not bring forth what is within
you, what you do not bring forth will destroy you.

—Gospel of Thomas

Respect yourself enough to walk away from anything that
no longer serves you, grows you, or makes you happy.

—Robert Tew

You are your greatest resource—invest wisely!

—Heidi Hanna

Believe in yourself and all that you are, know that there is
something inside you that is greater than any obstacle.

—Christian D. Larson

Change the World

Most of us will never get a Nobel Peace Prize, a Pulitzer Prize, or an Olympic gold medal. Few will ever become household names. Still, each and every one of us can make a difference in the world.

I've met people who are excellent cooks and change the world by sharing the love they put into their food. I've meet people who are good listeners and others who are great huggers; they change people's lives by their caring, comforting, and compassion. I've also met people who are very talented and help bring beauty and joy into the world through their artwork.

It need not be some grand undertaking to make a difference. Sometimes it can be the smallest of things. Reminding someone how much you love and appreciate them, for example, can help lift someone up who is feeling down. Being the best dad or mom you can be will make a huge difference in a child's life. Making someone's day with a smile, holding the door open for them, or complimenting them might make more of a difference then we will ever know.

As the first few quotations in this section state, it doesn't take much to change the world.

Change the world today. Start with the next person you meet.

—Dillon Burroughs

Together we can change the world, just one
random act of kindness at a time.

—Ron Hall

Let us remember: One book, one pen, one child,
and one teacher can change the world.

—Malala Yousafzai

Wishes don't change the world. Only actions will do that job.

—Israelmore Ayivor

You can't make footprints in the sands of time
by sitting on your butt. And who wants to
leave buttprints in the sands of time?

—Bob Moawad

We must not be afraid to reveal the rainbow
buried deep within us, to spread our wings
and help make the world flourish.

—Chip St. Clair

Never doubt that a small group of thoughtful,
committed citizens can change the world;
indeed, it's the only thing that ever has.

—Margaret Mead

Be the change that you want to see in the world.

—Mahatma Gandhi

If you want to see real change, stay persistent in educating
humanity on how similar we all are rather than how
different. Don't only strive to be the change you want to
see in the world, but also help all those around you see
the world through commonalities of the heart so that
they would want to change with you…. The language
of the heart is mankind's main common language.

—Suzy Kassem

Human potential is amazing…. We have the capacity
to create a world that is peaceful…one that spreads
kindness and love rather than hatred. If we believe it
to be so, it will be our truth, and we will create it.

—Kristi Bowman

Let the power of your love change the world, but never let
the problems of this world change the beauty of your love.

—Debasish Mridha

How to change the world:
spread positivity
bring people up instead of dragging them down
treat others the way you wish to be treated.

—Germany Kent

There is no exercise better for the heart than
reaching down and lifting people up.

—John Andrew Holmes, Jr.

Remember, if you ever need a helping hand, you'll
find one at the end of your arm.... As you grow older
you will discover that you have two hands: one for
helping yourself, the other for helping others.

—Audrey Hepburn

Whoever changes one life, changes the whole world

—Michele Amitrani

When you set out to change the world, the job seems
insurmountable, but each of us can do his or her small part
to effect change. We change the world when we choose to
create a world of forgiveness in our own hearts and minds.

—Desmond Tutu

My friends, love is better than anger. Hope is better than
fear. Optimism is better than despair. So let us be loving,
hopeful, and optimistic. And we'll change the world.

—Jack Layton

In every day, there are 1,440 minutes. That means we have 1,440 daily opportunities to make a positive impact.

—Les Brown

The most powerful thing you can do to change the world is to change your own beliefs about the nature of life, people, reality, to something more positive.

—Shakti Gawain

Change your thoughts and you change your world.

—Norman Vincent Peale

Having a positive attitude gives you the power to uplift, the power to create change, the power to motivate, the power to inspire, the power to influence, the power to cultivate happiness, and the list goes on.

—Lindsey Rietzsch

You are not here merely to make a living. You are
here in order to enable the world to live more amply,
with greater vision, with a finer spirit of hope and
achievement. You are here to enrich the world, and
you impoverish yourself if you forget the errand.

—Woodrow Wilson

We are here not to Make Money.
We are here to Make a Difference.

—Pratyay Amrit

We ourselves feel that what we are doing is
just a drop in the ocean. But the ocean would
be less because of that missing drop.

—Mother Teresa

I think the purpose of life is to be useful, to be
responsible, to be honorable, to be compassionate. It
is, after all, to matter: to count, to stand for something,
to have made some difference that you lived at all.

—Leo Rosten

It only takes one voice, at the right
pitch, to start an avalanche.

—Dianna Hardy

If you think you are too small to make a
difference, try sleeping with a mosquito.

—Dalai Lama

In every community, there is work to be done. In every
nation, there are wounds to heal.
In every heart, there is the power to do it.

—Marianne Williamson

Do not be dismayed by the brokenness of the world.
All things break. And all things can be mended. Not
with time, as they say, but with intention. So go. Love
intentionally, extravagantly, unconditionally. The broken
world waits in darkness for the light that is you.

—L. R. Knost

The future is unlimited for you right now; no one
can know what you are capable of. Do not surrender!
Only you are capable of changing the world.

—Kamal Khanzada

The secret of change is to focus all of your energy,
not on fighting the old, but on building the new.

—Dan Millman

Every great dream begins with a dreamer. Always remember,
you have within you the strength, the patience, and the
passion to reach for the stars to change the world.

—Anonymous

If you want to change the world, start off by making your
bed. If you have a miserable day, you will come home
to a bed that is made. That you made. And a made bed
gives you encouragement that tomorrow will be better.

—William H. McRaven

Cultivate Compassion

In the past, I hardly ever gave money to a homeless person. I'm not proud of that, but it was part of my upbringing during World War II. There was a scarcity mentality in my family, in part, I think, because many things were rationed during the war.

I've since gone beyond that lack thinking and now get a sense of pleasure knowing that, by giving, I can help others. But for a long while there was something missing whenever I gave money to a homeless person. I felt a separation between them and me, a kind of "have" and "have-not." And sometimes, even some annoyance, when they didn't thank me for my donation.

More recently, a simple gesture helped me change my uneasiness. It increased my compassion and helped us bond in some small way. Instead of dropping some money in their cup or handing the cash to them and then walking on, I now stop and ask their name. In return, they often ask me mine. Sometimes the conversation continues, but even when it doesn't, the simple act of asking their name helps us connect on a deeper, more compassionate, level.

Ignite the fire of loving kindness in your soul, fuel
that fire with understanding and compassion for
others, and start a bonfire of love worldwide.

—Nanette Mathews

Live through love, live as love and miracles happen. The
greatest miracle is that love gives you passion. When
passion and love meet, they become compassion.

—Pragito Dove

The individual is capable of both great compassion
and great indifference. He has it within his means
to nourish the former and outgrow the latter.

—Norman Cousins

When the power of love will replace the love of power,
then will our world know the blessings of peace.

—William Ewart Gladstone (attributed)

Something amazing happens when we surrender and just love. We melt into another world, a realm of power already within us. The world changes when we change. The world softens when we soften. The world loves us when we choose to love the world.

—Marianne Williamson

Love is the greatest healing power I know. Love can heal even the deepest and most painful memories because love brings the light of understanding to the darkest corners of our hearts and minds.

—Louise Hay

We need love in our hearts so we don't perpetuate a cycle of anger and hate, but we need fierceness so that we don't let things continue on their current harmful path.

—Dr. Kristin Neff

Whenever you are confronted with an opponent, conquer him with love.

—Mahatma Gandhi

Hatred does not cease by hatred, but only
by love; this is the eternal rule.

—The Buddha

Until you have learned to be tolerant with those who
do not always agree with you; until you have cultivated
the habit of saying some kind word of those whom
you do not admire; until you have formed the habit
of looking for the good instead of the bad there is in
others, you will be neither successful nor happy.

—Napoleon Hill

Everything that irritates us about others can
lead us to an understanding of ourselves.

—Carl Jung

When it comes to people who disagree with us, instead
of calling them names, call them up for coffee.

—Jason Kotecki

Open the window to your heart…. Release all the
warm, genuine love you hold inside so that it may
shine on others and shatter the darkness.

—Nanette Mathews

You will see in the world what you carry in your heart.

—Creig Crippen

Your heart, the compassionate part of you, knows that it's
impossible to feel better at the expense of someone else.

—Richard Carlson

Become more accepting. With every interaction,
surrender any tendency to judge another
person. Pray for a more accepting heart.

—Marianne Williamson

When we hear another person's feelings and
needs, we recognize our common humanity.

—Marshall Rosenberg

Empathy begins with understanding life from another
person's perspective. Nobody has an objective experience
of reality. It's all through our own individual prisms.

—Sterling K. Brown

It's only in our minds that we are separate
from the rest of the world.

—Gay Luce

Wait long enough and people will surprise and impress.
When you're pissed off at someone and you're angry at them,
you just haven't given them enough time. Just give them a
little more time and they almost always will impress you.

—Randy Pausch

Be nice to people on your way up because
you'll meet them on your way down.

—Wilson Mizner

Never look down on anybody unless you're helping them up.

—Jesse Jackson

If you step on people in this life
you're going to come back as a cockroach.

—Willie Davis

You have it easily in your power to increase the sum
total of this world's happiness now. How? By giving
a few words of sincere appreciation to someone who
is lonely or discouraged. Perhaps you will forget
tomorrow the kind words you say today, but the
recipient may cherish them over a lifetime.

—Dale Carnegie

A pat on the back, though only a few vertebrae removed
from a kick in the pants, is miles ahead in results.

—Bennett Cerf

Kindness is a hard thing to give away; it
keeps coming back to the giver.

—Ralph Scott

Kindness is in our power, even when fondness is not.

—Samuel Johnson

Kind words can be short and easy to speak,
but their echoes are truly endless.

—Mother Teresa

Shall we make a new rule of life from tonight: always
to try to be a little kinder than is necessary?

—J. M. Barrie

Dare to Dream

After my wife, who had a great sense of humor, died at an early age, I wanted to share how helpful therapeutic humor was for me both during and after my loss. The trouble was, I was way too nervous to ever get up and speak in front of a group. In fact, I almost failed speech in college.

I cried a lot during my wife's terminal diagnosis, but there was also laughter that helped me rise above the situation and get on with my life. Nobody was discussing the importance of humor in death and dying situations. My passion, my dream, was to share that important information.

Someone told me about the National Speakers Association, but I was reluctant to go to their meetings. Then one day, probably while I was in the shower, I thought that the best way to become a professional speaker was to hang around with others who were already successful at doing what I wanted to do.

I joined NSA and learned, among other valuable information, how to put my public speaking fear behind me and focus on my subject matter. The rest is history. For almost thirty years, I've been a successful award-winning professional speaker, in spite of the fact that I was once scared stiff of speaking in public.

The biggest adventure you can take is
to live the life of your dreams.

—Oprah Winfrey

So many of our dreams at first seem impossible,
then they seem improbable, and then, when we
summon the will, they soon become inevitable.

—Christopher Reeve

Keep your dreams alive. Understand that to achieve
anything requires faith and belief in yourself, vision,
hard work, determination, and dedication. Remember
all things are possible for those who believe.

—Gail Devers

Never let the odds keep you from doing what you
know in your heart you were meant to do.

—H. Jackson Brown, Jr.

Reach high, for stars lie hidden in you. Dream
deep, for every dream precedes the goal.

—Rabindranath Tagore

Put your future in good hands—your own.

—Mark Victor Hansen

People with goals succeed because they
know where they're going.

—Earl Nightingale

Your goals, minus your doubts, equal your reality.

—Ralph Marston

Never underestimate the power of dreams and the influence
of the human spirit. We are all the same in this notion:
The potential for greatness lives within each of us.

—Wilma Rudolph

Dreams are the seeds of change. Nothing ever grows without a seed, and nothing ever changes without a dream.

—Debby Boone

If you can dream it, you can do it.

—Walt Disney

Decide what you want, decide what you are willing to exchange for it. Establish your priorities and go to work.

—H. L. Hunt

Stay true to yourself, yet always be open to learn. Work hard, and never give up on your dreams, even when nobody else believes they can come true but you. These are not clichés but real tools you need no matter what you do in life to stay focused on your path.

—Phillip Sweet

No person has the right to rain on your dreams.

—Marian Wright Edelman

And those who were seen dancing were thought to
be crazy by those who could not hear the music.

—Anonymous

Dream big and chase your dreams—hold on to
optimism—even in failure, amazing things will happen!

—Bill Clinton

You see things; and you say, "Why?" But I dream
things that never were; and I say, "Why not?"

—George Bernard Shaw

Never give up on what you really want to do. The person with
big dreams is more powerful than the one with all the facts.

—H. Jackson Brown, Jr.

No one should negotiate their dreams. Dreams must be free to fly high. No government, no legislature, has a right to limit your dreams. You should never agree to surrender your dreams.

—Jesse Jackson

So many people will tell you "no," and you need to find something you believe in so hard that you just smile and tell them "watch me." Learn to take rejection as motivation to prove people wrong. Be unstoppable. Refuse to give up, no matter what. It's the best skill you can ever learn.

—Charlotte Eriksson

Far away there in the sunshine are my highest aspirations. I may not reach them, but I can look up and see their beauty, believe in them, and try to follow where they lead.

—Louisa May Alcott

If you are working on something that you really care about, you don't have to be pushed. The vision pulls you.

—Steve Jobs

When you have a dream, you've got
to grab it and never let go.

—Carol Burnett

If your ship doesn't come in, swim out to it.

—Jonathan Winters

If one dream should fall and break into a
thousand pieces, never be afraid to pick one
of those pieces up and begin again.

—Flavia Weedn

I'm a dreamer. I have to dream and reach for the stars,
and if I miss a star then I grab a handful of clouds.

—Mike Tyson

When you cease to dream, you cease to live.

—Malcolm Forbes

It is better to risk starving to death then surrender.
If you give up on your dreams, what's left?

—Jim Carrey

What would you attempt to do if you
knew you could not fail?

—Robert H. Schuller

Because a door slammed shut, we assume that our
dreams were slammed shut with it. Yet before we
surrender to a closed door, it might be wise to take
a moment and consider the fact that any dream is
far too big not to have a couple of back doors.

—Craig D. Lounsbrough

Twenty years from now, you will be more disappointed by
the things that you didn't do than by the ones you did do,
so throw off the bowlines, sail away from safe harbor, catch
the trade winds in your sails. Explore, dream, discover.

—Sarah Frances Brown

Never underestimate the power of dreams and the influence
of the human spirit. We are all the same in this notion:
The potential for greatness lives within each of us.

—Wilma Rudolph

Throw your dreams into space like a kite, and
you do not know what it will bring back, a new
life, a new friend, a new love, a new country.

—Anaïs Nin

Have Hope

According to the dictionary, one of the definitions for the word "hope" is "a desire for a certain thing to happen." And that is exactly what occurred just before my recent trip to New York City.

Having grown up there, I know that August is not the best time to be on the East Coast. The weather can be hot, humid, and oppressive. But the apartment where we often stay was only available then, so we went.

Several weeks before we left for the Big Apple, I wrote a "Hope Note"—a positive affirmation that read:

   NYC Weather: August 21 to August 28.
   Cool and clear. 73 to 83 degrees every day.

I thought that if a weatherman could predict the weather and be right only some of the time, I could create my own forecast and perhaps have a higher batting average than they have. And guess what? I did.

For six out of the eight days we were there, we had low humidity with temperatures never going above eighty-five. It only rained one time, and that was in the middle of the night. Two days out of the eight were hot and humid, but one of those was on the day we were leaving.

My positive affirmation worked. No, I do not think I can predict the weather, but writing down what I wanted to have happen accomplished several things. It gave me hope for what might be possible, it affirmed what I wanted to have happen, and it provided a positive outlook, which helped ease any anxiety about the weather. And all of this because of my little "Hope Note."

To travel hopefully is a better thing than to arrive.

—Robert Louis Stevenson

We begin to realize that it will take something more powerful than we are to relieve our suffering. This is what we've been missing all along—a source of hope.

—Marta Mrotek

Hope is the feeling you have that the feeling you have isn't permanent.

—Jean Kerr

They say a person needs just three things to be truly happy in this world. Someone to love, something to do, and something to hope for.

—Tom Bodett

The important thing is not that we can live on hope alone, but that life is not worth living without it.

—Harvey Milk

If you lose hope, somehow you lose the vitality that keeps life moving, you lose that courage to be, that quality that helps you to go on in spite of it all.

—Dr. Martin Luther King, Jr.

Look not thou down but up!

—Robert Browning

Most of the important things in the world have been accomplished by people who have kept on trying when there seemed to be no hope at all.

—Dale Carnegie

It is difficult to say what is impossible, for the dream of yesterday is the hope of today and the reality of tomorrow.

—Robert H. Goddard

I've interviewed and portrayed people who've withstood some of the ugliest things life can throw at you, but the one quality all of them seem to share is an ability to maintain hope for a brighter morning, even during our darkest nights.

—Oprah Winfrey

The struggle you're in today is developing the strength you need tomorrow.

—Robert Tew

Though no one can backtrack and create a brand-new start, everyone is capable of taking their life in a brand-new direction.

—Germany Kent

As I look back on my life, I realize that every time I thought I was being rejected from something good, I was actually being redirected to something better.

—Steve Maraboli

If we convince ourselves that there is no hope,
our subconscious mind edits out of the picture
any evidence that might prove otherwise.

—Marianne Williamson

There are no hopeless situations; there are only
people who have grown hopeless about them.

—Clare Boothe Luce

The hopeful man sees success where others see failure,
sunshine where others see shadows and storm.

—Orison S. Marden

If winter comes, can spring be far behind?

—Percy Bysshe Shelley

After all, tomorrow is another day.

—Margaret Mitchell

I have always been delighted at the prospect of a new day, a fresh try, one more start, with perhaps a bit of magic waiting somewhere behind the morning.

—J. B. Priestly

Hope is a renewable option: If you run out of it at the end of the day, you get to start over in the morning.

—Barbara Kingsolver

Hope is being able to see that there is light despite all of the darkness.

—Desmond Tutu

Hope is a helium balloon. It is a wish lantern set out into the dark sky of night.

—Sharon Weil

Hope is the power of being cheerful in circumstances that we know to be desperate.

—G. K. Chesterton

Hope begins in the dark, the stubborn hope that if you just show up and try to do the right thing, the dawn will come. You wait and watch and work: you don't give up.

—Anne Lamott

Hope itself is like a star—not to be seen in the sunshine of prosperity, and only to be discovered in the night of adversity.

—Charles Haddon Spurgeon

Once you choose hope, anything's possible.

—Christopher Reeve

When you're at the end of your rope, tie a knot and hold on.

—Theodore Roosevelt

What is hope but a feeling of optimism, a thought that says things will improve, it won't always be bleak, there's a way to rise above the present circumstances.

—Wayne Dyer

Hope is important because it can make the present moment less difficult to bear. If we believe that tomorrow will be better, we can bear a hardship today.

—Thich Nhat Hanh

We must accept finite disappointment, but we must never lose infinite hope.

—Dr. Martin Luther King, Jr.

Never lose hope. Storms make people stronger and never last forever.

—Roy T. Bennett

The best way to not feel hopeless is to get up and do something. Don't wait for good things to happen to you. If you go out and make some good things happen, you will fill the world with hope, you will fill yourself with hope.

—Barack Obama

Never give up hope. All things are working for
your good. One day, you'll look back on everything
you've been through and thank God for it.

—Germany Kent

Keep hope alive!

—Jesse Jackson

Learn to Forgive

When I was growing up, we lived on the fifth floor of an apartment house in the Bronx. There were eight apartments to a floor. I don't know exactly what happened, but one day my mother and a next-door neighbor had a huge fight. It continued for several years and included the neighbor throwing shoe polish at our clothes, which hung on our clothesline outside her window. It also resulted in my not being able to ever speak to, or play with, her son again.

It puzzled me why my family never made up with them. Even at that young age, I realized that not forgiving created an uncomfortable feeling and a weight that I carried around the entire time we lived there.

One teacher I read about demonstrated exactly what I was feeling when my family refused to forgive a neighbor. The teacher gave each student a sack and some potatoes. She then had them write the names of people they hadn't forgiven on each potato. Then she told them to put the potatoes in the sack and carry them around the room. Pretty soon the burden of carrying around the weight of someone they hadn't forgiven became very clear.

Perhaps a few of the quotations below will help you forgive someone and release the burden you've been lugging around with you.

Life is too short for long-term grudges.

—Elon Musk

To carry a grudge is like being stung to death by one bee.

—William H. Walton

The truth is, unless you let go, unless you forgive yourself,
unless you forgive the situation, unless you realize that
the situation is over, you cannot move forward.

—Steve Maraboli

When you hold resentment toward another, you are
bound to that person or condition by an emotional
link that is stronger than steel. Forgiveness is the
only way to dissolve that link and get free.

—Catherine Ponder

Forgive and let go. Not necessarily because those
who mistreated you deserve it, but because you do.
Let forgiveness liberate you from your past. Allow it
to take away all the resentment you've kept in your
heart for all this time, and allow it to fill in that empty
space with love. Forgive, release, and let go.

—Luminita D. Saviuc

Without forgiveness, life is governed by an
endless cycle of resentment and retaliation.

—Roberto Assagioli

Resentment is one burden that is incompatible
with your success. Always be the first to
forgive; and forgive yourself first always.

—Dan Zadra

To err is human; to forgive, divine.

—Alexander Pope

If you haven't forgiven yourself something,
how can you forgive others?

—Dolores Huerta

Being gentle means forgiving yourself when you mess
up. We should learn from our mistakes, but we shouldn't
beat the tar out of ourselves over them. He that cannot
forgive others breaks the bridge over which he must
pass himself; for every man has need to be forgiven.

—Thomas Fuller

Forgive, and ye shall be forgiven.

—Luke 6:37

The past is just that, past. Learn what went wrong and why.
Make amends if you need to. Then drop it and move on.

—Sean Covey

When a man points a finger at someone else, he should
remember that three of his fingers are pointing at himself.

—Anonymous

Try to forgive by trying to understand how it
would feel to be in the other's shoes.

—Jay Woodman

One forgives to the degree that one loves.

—La Rochefoucauld

Forgiveness is the final form of love.

—Reinhold Niebuhr

Life is an adventure in forgiveness.

—Norman Cousins

We may not know how to forgive, and we may not want to forgive; but the very fact we say we are willing to forgive begins the healing practice.

—Louise Hay

When a deep injury is done us, we never recover until we forgive.

—Alan Paton

When I am able to resist the temptation to judge others, I can see them as teachers of forgiveness in my life, reminding me that I can only have peace of mind when I forgive rather than judge.

—Gerald Jampolsky

Keeping score of old scores and scars, getting even, and one-upping always make you less than you are.

—Malcolm Forbes

Any man can seek revenge; it takes a
king or prince to grant a pardon.

—Arthur J. Rehrat

Anger makes you smaller, while forgiveness
forces you to grow beyond what you were.

—Chérie Carter-Scott

Always forgive your enemies—nothing
annoys them so much.

—Oscar Wilde

Forgiveness is a funny thing.
It warms the heart and cools the sting.

—William Arthur Ward

Forgiveness is the magnet which draws your
endless good. It wipes clean the slate of the
past to let you receive in the present.

—Catherine Ponder

To forgive is to refuse to contaminate the
future with the errors of the past.

—Craig D. Lounsbrough

Forgiveness is not always easy. At times, it feels more
painful than the wound we suffered to forgive the one that
inflicted it. And yet, there is no peace without forgiveness.

—Marianne Williamson

Silently repeat to yourself: I forgive myself for any
ways in which I knowingly or unknowingly caused
hurt or harm to any living being or creature.

—Michael Bernard Beckwith

Let It Go

Okay, I'll admit it. I'm a worrier. Well, maybe not a fulltime worrier, but someone who gets more anxious about things than perhaps need be. I think it stems from my being an overachiever in the planning department. Then, when things don't work out as I planned, I get anxious.

But there is something I learned from Unity of San Francisco, the spiritual center I attend, and their New Thought teachings. It has helped me lower my self-created anxiety. One of their teachings is, "Let Go, Let God."

Their interpretation of God is that it is something that is both all around us and in everything, including ourselves. Thus, when I need to let go of my anxiety, I am not asking some outside force to change me but asking the God within to help me let go of my anxious moments.

It has been very empowering and comforting to know that I, the God within, have the power to release my troubling moments and the power to help me let go of what no longer serves me.

I hope that the Unity teaching about letting go will help you too. If not, or in addition to that, perhaps the powerful thoughts below will help you release that which is holding you back from a full and rich life.

Learn to let go. That is the key to happiness.

—The Buddha

The bird of paradise alights only upon
the hand that does not grasp.

—John Berry

Some of us think holding on makes us
strong; but sometimes it is letting go.

—Hermann Hesse

Focus on the highest, clearest, and most meaningful
teaching you can find, and let all else go.

—Alan Cohen

All the art of living lies in a fine mingling
of letting go and holding on.

—Havelock Ellis

We all have 100 percent to deal with in our lives.
10 percent is important, 90 percent unimportant.
The secret to a happy, productive life is to deal
with the 10 percent and let the 90 percent slip.

—Salli Rasberry and Padi Selwyn

Let go of your perceived control,
and let the unknown turn you on.

—Preston Smiles

If we can just let go and trust that things will work
out the way they're supposed to without trying to
control the outcome, then we can begin to enjoy the
moment more fully. The joy of the freedom it brings
becomes more pleasurable than the experience itself.

—Goldie Hawn

Letting go is not about giving up, being lazy, or
sacrificing yourself… Letting go doesn't have to
mean losing; it can be about coming into a new,
open, clean space from which you can create.

—Rebekah Elizabeth Gamble

Surrender to the flow.

—Mike Gordon

Detachment creates room for creation.

—Tosha Silver

The more you go with the flow of life and
surrender the outcome to God, and the less you
seek constant clarity, the more you will find that
fabulous things start to show up in your life.

—Mandy Hale

Surrender is when we stop toiling and striving and we
begin receiving and arriving. Nothing is more beautiful
to experience than the inner rest that follows surrender.

—Shannon Tanner

Allow yourself to let go, surrender, and breathe
in the beautiful world that is waiting for you
just outside of your comfort zone.

—Leigh Hershkovich

In order to pick something up,
you've got to put something down.

—Todd Stocker

The truth is, unless you let go, unless you forgive yourself,
unless you forgive the situation, unless you realize that
the situation is over, you cannot move forward.

—Steve Maraboli

Let go of those thoughts that do not serve you anymore.

—Debasish Mridha

Fear and guilt are your enemies. If you let go of fear, fear lets go of you. If you release guilt, guilt will release you. How do you do that? By choosing to. It's that simple.

—Donald L. Hicks

Letting go helps us live in a more peaceful state of mind and helps restore our balance. It allows others to be responsible for themselves and lets us take our hands off situations that do not belong to us. This frees us from unnecessary stress.

—Melody Beattie

Suffering is not holding you. You are holding suffering. When you become good at the art of letting suffering go, then you'll come to realize how unnecessary it was for you to drag those burdens around with you. You'll see that no one else other than you was responsible. The truth is that existence wants your life to become a festival.

—Osho

Letting go means to come to the realization that some people are a part of your history, but not a part of your destiny.

—Steve Maraboli

If there are people you haven't forgiven, you're not
going to really awaken. You have to let go.

—Eckhart Tolle

Holding on to anger hurts no one but yourself.

—Marianne Williamson

When we hate our enemies, we are giving them power
over us: power over our sleep, our appetites, our blood
pressure, our health, and our happiness. Our enemies
would dance with joy if only they knew how they were
worrying us, lacerating us, and getting even with us!
Our hate is not hurting them at all, but our hate is
turning our days and nights into a hellish turmoil.

—Dale Carnegie

When you release the negative experiences that are
behind you, it makes room for love to move in. It's as easy
as a decision. God is patiently waiting for your reply.

—Pam Malow-Isham

Breathe. Let go. And remind yourself that this very moment is the only one you know you have for sure.

—Oprah Winfrey

It takes a lot of courage to release the familiar and seemingly secure, to embrace the new. But there is no real security in what is no longer meaningful. There is more security in the adventurous and exciting, for in movement there is life, and in change there is power.

—Alan Cohen

What is given to you is what is needed; what you *want* requires giving up what you don't need.

—George Alexiou

If it comes, let it come. If it goes, it's okay, let it go. Let things come and go. Stay calm, don't let anything disturb your peace, and carry on.

—Germany Kent

Even though you may want to move forward in your life, you may have one foot on the brakes. In order to be free, we must learn how to let go. Release the hurt. Release the fear. Refuse to entertain your old pain. The energy it takes to hang onto the past is holding you back from a new life. What is it you would let go of today?

—Mary Manin Morrissey

Lighten Up

When I was writing my first book, *The Healing Power of Humor*, I would close my office door in order to concentrate on my work and to avoid being disturbed. At the time, my daughter was in her early teens. She would often knock on the door and enter before I could respond. Usually she wanted to talk about something that could have waited until I took a break.

After she had interrupted me several times one morning, I put a big sign on the door that read, "Do Not Disturb Unless It's an Emergency."

No sooner than I posted the sign than there was another knock. This time I was really annoyed and shouted, "Is this an emergency?"

"Yes," she replied softly.

"Okay," I angrily got up and opened the door. "What is it?" I shouted.

She said, "I forgot to tell you I love you."

Tears welled up in my eyes as I realized that I was taking my writing and myself too seriously. What irony! Here I was writing a book about the value of therapeutic humor and I had lost my own sense of humor.

It took my young daughter to teach me a lesson in lightening up. Hopefully some of the quotes below will do the same for you.

Find a place inside where there's joy,
and the joy will burn out the pain.

—Joseph Campbell

Life would be tragic if it weren't funny.

—Stephen Hawking

A sense of humor helps us to get through the dull
times, cope with the difficult times, enjoy the
good times, and manage the scary times.

—Steve Goodier

A person without a sense of humor is like a wagon
without springs—jolted by every pebble in the road.

—Henry Ward Beecher

Against the assault of laughter, nothing can stand.

—Mark Twain

I have always set personal boundaries of what is funny
and what is not. I have been quoted as saying, "There
are just some things you don't poke fun at." I was
wrong. Laughter rises out of tragedy when you need
it the most and rewards you for your courage.

—Erma Bombeck

Humor is the great thing, the saving thing, after all. The
moment it arises, all our hardnesses yield, all our irritations
and resentments flit away, and a sunny spirit takes their place.

—Mark Twain

Angels can fly because they take themselves lightly.

—G. K. Chesterton

Let your life lightly dance on the edges of
time like dew on the tip of a leaf.

—Rabindranath Tagore

The one important thing I've learned over the years is the difference between taking one's work seriously and one's self seriously. The first is imperative; the second is disastrous.

—Dame Margot Fonteyn

Do not take life too seriously.
You will never get out of it alive.

—Elbert Hubbard

Learn to enjoy every minute of your life. Be happy now. Don't wait for something outside of yourself to make you happy in the future. Think how really precious is the time you have to spend, whether it's at work or with your family. Every minute should be enjoyed and savored.

—Earl Nightingale

Life is filled with tragedy, with long patches of struggle and with, I think, beautiful bursts of joy and accomplishment. Blessed with those moments, you just try to relax as much as possible and focus on the little things, like the joy of changing your baby's diaper.

—David Dastmalchian

Sorrow digs the well and joy fills it.

—Randy Peyser

When we can laugh through our tears, we are
being given a powerful message. Things may
be bad, but they cannot be all that bad.

—Allen Klein

I live by this credo: Have a little laugh and look
around you for happiness instead of sadness. Laughter
has always brought me out of unhappy situations.
Even in your darkest moment, you usually can find
something to laugh about if you try hard enough.

—Red Skelton

I liken laughter to a stream of light that can
filter through any darkened space. It just needs a
crack to enter, and then, like magic, it effortlessly
penetrates and overshadows the darkness.

—Ros Ben-Moshe

If you're going to be able to look back on something and
laugh about it, you might as well laugh about it now.

—Marie Osmond

Dragging around pain and attachments from the past
can jeopardize your health, your relationships, and
your happiness. It can undermine your motivation,
discourage your progress, and make everything in
life harder. What can you release to simplify your
life, lighten your load, and find more joy?

—Susan C. Young

Although a lot can be learned from adversity, most of the
same lessons can be learned through laughter and joy.

—John-Roger and Peter McWilliams

Do you want a world…with more joy and happiness?
Then find your own joy and happiness and
contribute to the joy and happiness of others.

—Bo Lozoff

Cheerfulness is contagious, but don't wait
to catch it from others. Be a carrier.

—Anonymous

A shared gift of laughter is a priceless gift to the spirit.

—Christine Clifford

You find yourself refreshed by the presence of cheerful
people. Why not make an honest effort to confer
that pleasure on others? Half the battle is gained if
you never allow yourself to say anything gloomy.

—Lydia M. Child

There's nothing more deadly to our ability to fight back
and resist than being deadly serious and solemn.

—Paula Vogel

We live in an ironic society where even play is
turned into work. But the highest existence is not
work; the highest level of existence is play.

—Conrad Hyers

Can you imagine experiencing the world as a great
sandbox given for us to play in like we did as children?

—Judith-Annette Milburn

We don't stop playing because we turn old,
but turn old because we stop playing.

—George Bernard Shaw

As kids, we danced all the time. We danced when we
were excited. We danced when we were happy. We even
danced when we were bored. Why did we ever stop?

—Jason Kotecki

There's power in looking silly and not caring that you do.

—Amy Poehler

What would our lives be like if our days were studded
by tiny, completely unproductive, silly, nonstrategic,
wild, and beautiful five-minute breaks, reminders
that our days are for loving and learning and
laughing, not for pushing and planning, reminders
that it's all about the heart, not about the hustle?

—Shauna Niequist

If you're reading this…Congratulations; you're alive. If that's
not something to smile about, then I don't know what is.

—Chad Sugg

Make Lemonade

There is an old expression that states, "When life hands you lemons, make lemonade." It is talking about turning not-so-great situations into something more positive.

I posted the first half of that cliché on Facebook and asked people to complete it. The responses were amazing, some humorous, some profound, all interesting. Here are some of the replies:

When life hands you lemons...

- throw them back
- juggle them
- paint them gold
- write a book about it
- ask if they're organic

Others wrote a short, lighthearted script that completed the sentence. This is from a colleague of mine, Joe Hoare:

> Give them back saying something pithy like, "No thank you. You mixed up your orders; these aren't what I ordered, because I've had them before, and as you agreed, it is time to branch out and experience something new and different—which is why, at your prompting, I ordered Sharon fruit. Why am I still waiting for them, purleeeeze?"

This section of quotations is about turning those sour situations in your life into more palatable ones. In other words, how to keep a positive and optimistic frame of mind during not-so-great times.

It's not what happens to you, but how you handle
it. If life gives you lemons, make lemonade. If
the lemons are rotten, take out the seeds and
plant them in order to grow new lemons.

—Louise Hay

You're going to go through tough times—that's
life. But I say, "Nothing happens to you, it happens
for you." See the positive in negative events.

—Joel Osteen

However mean your life is, meet it and live it; do not shun
it and call it bad names. It is not so bad as you are. The
faultfinder will find fault even in paradise. Love your life.

—Henry David Thoreau

When life gives you lemons don't make lemonade,
make pink lemonade. Be unique.

—Wanda Sykes

Whenever a negative thought concerning your personal power comes to mind, deliberately voice a positive thought to cancel it out.

—Norman Vincent Peale

When life gives you lemons, make lemonade and sell it to all of those who get thirsty from complaining.

—Napoleon Hill

Once you replace negative thoughts with positive ones, you'll start having positive results.

—Willie Nelson

Every good thought you think is contributing its share to the ultimate result of your life.

—Grenville Kleiser

Positive thinking is more than just a tagline. It changes the way we behave. And I firmly believe that when I am positive, it not only makes me better, but it also makes those around me better.

—Harvey Mackay

I believe that if life gives you lemons, you should make lemonade…and try to find somebody whose life has given them vodka, and have a party.

—Ron White

Despite what might seem to be the saddest and most intractable situation, we have the power to believe that something else is possible, that things can change, that a miracle can happen.

—Marianne Williamson

Successful people maintain a positive focus in life no matter what is going on around them.

—Jack Canfield

Optimism is a happiness magnet. If you stay positive,
good things and good people will be drawn to you.

—Mary Lou Retton

When life throws you lemons, you make lemonade.
When life throws you trash, throw it out.

—Bonnie Zackson Koury

It's vital to our survival to be positive.

—Lindsey Rietzsch

Pessimism leads to weakness, optimism to power.

—William James

We are all in the gutter, but some of
us are looking at the stars.

—Oscar Wilde

When life gives you lemons, make lemonade, and then
throw it in the face of the person who gave you the lemons
until they give you the oranges you originally asked for.

—Cassandra Clare

The true optimist not only expects the best to happen, but
goes to work to make the best happen. The true optimist not
only looks upon the bright side but trains every force that
is in him to produce more and more brightness in his life.

—Christian D. Larson

Optimism is the faith that leads to achievement.
Nothing can be done without hope and confidence.

—Helen Keller

Few things in the world are more powerful than
a positive push: a smile, a world of optimism and
hope, a "you can do it" when things are tough.

—Richard M. Devos

When life gives you lemons, make grape juice and
sit back and watch the world ask how you did it.

—Tori Truax

If you are positive, you'll see opportunities
instead of obstacles.

—Widad Akrawi

In times of great stress or adversity, it's always
best to keep busy, to plow your anger and
your energy into something positive.

—Lee Iacocca

If you absolutely can't stay positive, don't go negative, just
cruise neutral for a while until you can get back up.

—Terri Guillemets

When life hands you lemons, make whisky sours.

—W. C. Fields

Here's the thing about reality. It isn't positive; it isn't negative.
It's neutral. You get to decide if it's positive or negative.

—Randy Gage

There is a basic law that like attracts like. Negative
thinking definitely attracts negative results. Conversely,
if a person habitually thinks optimistically and hopefully,
his positive thinking sets in motion positive forces—and
success, instead of eluding him, flows toward him.

—Norman Vincent Peale

Never Give Up

In another section of this book, I write about wanting to be a theatrical scenic designer and then many years later being asked to leave the school where I was studying to become one. Although I was devastated at the time, I never gave up on my pursuit.

The journey was not easy, and there were many obstacles in the way, but I was determined to make my dream come true; I never gave up.

My path included doing department store window displays, designing ten shows in ten weeks in summer stock, washing out paint buckets at a scenic painting shop, becoming an apprentice in television, and finally, taking a very difficult month-long union test. I failed on my first attempt. But I joyously passed on my second try, which meant that I was a full-fledged, bona fide, card-carrying scenic designer.

Each of us has a different path and different goals. More often than not, there will be naysayers along the way. Most likely there will also be obstacles along the way. Don't listen to people who try and keep you from your dreams. Rise above any stumbling blocks. Keep on going. Never give up.

You may be the only person left who believes
in you, but it's enough. It takes just one star to
pierce a universe of darkness. Never give up.

—Richelle E. Goodrich

I think a hero is an ordinary individual who
finds the strength to persevere and endure
in spite of overwhelming obstacles.

—Christopher Reeve

Keep on keepin' on.

—Saying

By perseverance the snail reached the ark.

—Charles Haddon Spurgeon

Little by little does the trick.

—Aesop

In the confrontation between the stream and
the rock, the stream always wins...not through
strength, but through persistence.

—Anonymous

Even the woodpecker owes his success to the
fact that he uses his head and keeps pecking
away until he finishes the job he starts.

—Coleman Cox

Nothing in the world can take the place of perseverance.
Talent will not... Genius will not... Education will not...
Perseverance and determination alone are omnipotent.

—Calvin Coolidge

Obstacles don't have to stop you. If you run into a
wall, don't turn around and give up. Figure out how
to climb it, go through it, or work around it.

—Michael Jordan

Don't get hung up on a snag in the stream, my dear. Snags alone are not so dangerous—it's the debris that clings to them that makes the trouble. Pull yourself loose and go on.

—Anne Shannon Monroe

We only have one rule. You can't stop. You can go as slow as you need to go, but you cannot stop. You can never drop out.

—Lewis Howes

Don't give up when you still have something to give. Nothing is really over until the moment you stop trying.

—Brian Dyson

Enjoy the good times and walk away from the bumps. Even failures can turn positive if you just keep going.

—Carl Reiner

A setback is the opportunity to begin again more intelligently.

—Henry Ford

Our greatest glory is not in never falling,
but in rising every time we fall.

—Confucius

Fall seven times, stand up eight.

—Japanese Proverb

When life knocks you down, try to land on your
back, because if you can look up, you can get up.

—Eric Thomas

The greatest glory in living lies not in never
failing, but in rising every time we fail.

—Nelson Mandela

My attitude has always been, if you fall flat on
your face, at least you're moving forward. All
you have to do is get back up and try again.

—Richard Branson

It is common sense to take a method and try it. If it fails, admit it frankly and try another. But above all, try something.

—Franklin D. Roosevelt

Problems are not stop signs; they are guidelines.

—Robert H. Schuller

You may be disappointed if you fail,
but you are doomed if you don't try.

—Beverly Sills

Many of life's failures are people who did not realize how close they were to success when they gave up.

—Thomas Edison

If you fell down yesterday, stand up today.

—H. G. Wells

If you were able to fall a hundred times as a child and rise,
you are able to fall a thousand times as a grown-up and soar.

—Matshona Dhliwayo

The habit of giving up when the present task is half finished
and trying something else is one of the chief causes of failure.

—Christian D. Larson

Remember that guy who gave up? Neither does anyone else.

—Anonymous

It's easy to have faith in yourself and have discipline when
you're a winner, when you're number one. What you got
to have is faith and discipline when you're not a winner.

—Vince Lombardi

Winning is great, sure, but if you are really going to do something in life, the secret is learning how to lose. Nobody goes undefeated all the time. If you can pick up after a crushing defeat and go on to win again, you are going to be a champion someday.

—Wilma Rudolph

It's not how hard you hit. It's how hard you get hit…and keep moving forward.

—Randy Pausch

Never confuse a single defeat with a final defeat.

—F. Scott Fitzgerald

You may encounter many defeats, but you must not be defeated. In fact, it may be necessary to encounter the defeats so you can know who you are, what you can rise from, how you can still come out of it.

—Maya Angelou

I do a lot of lectures on survival. I always say you can't change what happened, so have a little wallow, feel very sorry for yourself, and then get up and move forward.

—Joan Rivers

Never let the odds keep you from doing what you know in your heart you were meant to do.

—H. Jackson Brown, Jr.

Set your goals high, and don't stop till you get there.

—Bo Jackson

When things go wrong, as they sometimes will,
when the road you're trudging seems all uphill,
when care is pressing you down a bit,
rest, if you must—but don't you quit.

—Anonymous

Growing up wrinkles the skin, giving up wrinkles the soul.

—Amit Kalantri

The slogan "Press On!" has solved and always
will solve the problems of the human race.

—Calvin Coolidge

Don't be discouraged. It's often the last key
in the bunch that opens the lock.

—Anonymous

Tough times never last, but tough people do.

—Robert H. Schuller

Practice Appreciation

A few years ago, I did an experiment. Each day of the year, I sent one email to someone thanking them for being in my life and telling them how much I appreciate them. I sent them to colleagues, neighbors, friends, and relatives. I sent them to people I had known for years and those who I'd met more recently.

When I first started doing this, I was a little concerned that I might run out of recipients later in the year. But I didn't. In fact, the more I thought about who I should send one of these emails to, the more people I recalled who I wanted to thank for being in my life.

What was so amazing, and what I never realized when I first started doing this, was the incredible feedback I got from the recipients. Many people responded how much they treasured my being part of their life. And several even told me that the timing was impeccable. They were having a difficult time and asked how I knew how much they needed to hear my message that someone appreciated them.

It was a simple idea that made an impact on other people's lives. But even more than that, it validated what I have learned throughout my years. The more I give, the more I get. And the more I am grateful for the things in my life, the more things for which to be grateful come into my life.

Appreciation is the highest form of prayer, for it acknowledges the presence of good wherever you shine the light of your thankful thoughts.

—Alan Cohen

By taking the time to stop and appreciate who you are and what you've achieved—and perhaps learned through a few mistakes, stumbles, and losses—you actually can enhance everything about you. Self-acknowledgment and appreciation are what give you the insights and awareness to move forward toward higher goals and accomplishments.

—Jack Canfield

It's ironic that when you go through a tragedy, you appreciate more. You realize how fragile life is and that there are still so many things for which to be thankful.

—Adam Grant

Hopeful thinking can get you out of your fear zone and into your appreciation zone.

—Martha Beck

Truly appreciate those around you, and you'll soon
find many others around you. Truly appreciate
life, and you'll find that you have more of it.

—Ralph Marston

As you waste your breath complaining about life,
someone out there is breathing their last. Appreciate
what you have. Be thankful and stop complaining. Live
more, complain less. Have more smiles, less stress.

—Anonymous

Be thankful for what you have; you'll end up
having more. If you concentrate on what you
don't have, you will never, ever have enough.

—Oprah Winfrey

It's a funny thing about life, once you begin to
take note of the things you are grateful for, you
begin to lose sight of the things that you lack.

—Germany Kent

To be upset over what you don't have
is to waste what you do have.

—Ken Keyes, Jr.

Too many people miss the silver lining
because they're expecting gold.

—Maurice Setter

Be grateful for what you already have while you pursue
your goals. If you aren't grateful for what you already have,
what makes you think you would be happy with more?

—Roy T. Bennett

Gratitude unlocks the fullness of life. It turns what
we have into enough, and more. It turns denial into
acceptance, chaos to order, confusion to clarity. It can
turn a meal into a feast, a house into a home, a stranger
into a friend. Gratitude makes sense of our past, brings
peace for today, and creates a vision for tomorrow.

—Melody Beattie

Gratitude is many things to many people. It is wondering; it is appreciation; it is looking at the bright side of a setback; it is fathoming abundance; it is thanking someone in your life; it is thanking God; it is "counting blessings."

—Sonja Lyubomirsky

Count your blessings, not your crosses,
Count your gains, not your losses.
Count your joys instead of your woes,
Count your friends instead of your foes.
Count your health, not your wealth.

—Proverb

When I started counting my blessings, my whole life turned around.

—Willie Nelson

I pray to start my day and finish it in prayer. I'm just thankful for everything, all the blessings in my life, trying to stay that way. I think that's the best way to start your day and finish your day. It keeps everything in perspective.

—Tim Tebow

The more grateful you are for everything good that comes
into your life, the more closely you place your mind in
contact with that power in life that can produce greater good.

—Christian D. Larson

Glow with gratitude and see how awe and
joy will make their home in you.

—Michael Bernard Beckwith

Gratitude is our most direct line to God and the angels.
If we take the time, no matter how crazy and troubled
we feel, we can find something to be thankful for. The
more we seek gratitude, the more reason the angels will
give us for gratitude and joy to exist in our lives.

—Terry Lynn Taylor

When life gets hectic and you feel overwhelmed,
take a moment to focus on the people and things you
are most grateful for. When you have an attitude of
gratitude, frustrating troubles will fall by the wayside.

—Dana Arcuri

Give thanks for a little and you will find a lot.

—Hausa Proverb

If you count all your assets, you always show a profit.

—Robert Quillen

If you want to turn your life around, try
thankfulness. It will change your life mightily.

—Gerald Good

If the only prayer you say in your whole life
is "thank you," that would suffice.

—Meister Eckhart

Feeling gratitude and not expressing it is like
wrapping a present and not giving it.

—William Arthur Ward

Here's the thing—none of us get out of life alive.
So be gallant, be great, be gracious, and be
grateful for the opportunities that you have.

—Jake Bailey

Give yourself a gift of five minutes of contemplation
in awe of everything you see around you. Go outside
and turn your attention to the many miracles around
you. This five-minute-a-day regimen of appreciation
and gratitude will help you to focus your life in awe.

—Wayne Dyer

As we express our gratitude, we must never forget that the
highest appreciation is not to utter words, but to live by them.

—John F. Kennedy

Put It in Perspective

Sometimes things aren't always the way they seem. One day, for example, I was walking my dog in Golden Gate Park in San Francisco. We came upon a beautiful emerald clearing. It was surrounded by lush ferns and moss. The patch of green looked like a deep-pile carpet. The grassy-looking texture was glistening in the sun and appeared soft and inviting.

I suspected it might be a moss-covered pond, but my dog thought otherwise. Excited at finding what looked like a good place to run, she immediately jumped on it. But it wasn't. It was a pool of water that was completely covered with green algae. Suddenly my formerly light-brown dog looked like she had been painted for St. Patrick's Day. And the expression on her face was priceless. She looked at me with disgust. I could almost hear her declaring, "What the (expletive)? Who put that soggy smelly gook there?"

It was a great lesson about how each of us may have a different perspective on the same situation. I saw a moss-covered pond. My dog saw a grassy area to frolic in—that is, until she literally tested the waters.

Our ancestors, who have already traversed this lifespan and
have seen what's beyond, have a different perspective than
we do. They are now able to see the big picture… Like us,
they experienced darkness, but they have received the gift
of perspective that allows them to see the beauty in it all.

—Jason Kotecki

Perspective gives us the ability to accurately contrast the large
with the small and the important with the less important.
Without it, we are lost in a world where all ideas, news,
and information look the same. We cannot differentiate,
we cannot prioritize, and we cannot make good choices.

—John Sununu

Time puts things in proper perspective.

—Cameron Crowe

The only thing you sometimes have control over is
perspective. You don't have control over your situation.
But you have a choice about how you view it.

—Chris Pine

We begin to learn wisely when we're willing to see
[the] world from other people's perspective.

—Toba Beta

You never really understand a person until you
consider things from his point of view.

—Harper Lee

The opinions of others are important. They are the yardstick
by which we measure our perspective on the world.

—Stewart Stafford

The climb might be tough and challenging, but
the view is worth it. There is a purpose for that
pain; you just can't always see it right away.

—Victoria Arlen

Life is supposed to be a series of peaks and valleys. The
secret is to keep the valleys from becoming Grand Canyons.

—Bernard Williams

Perspective is as simple as answering this
question: If I had five months to live, would
I experience this problem differently?

—Shannon L. Alder

It suddenly struck me that that tiny pea, pretty and
blue, was the Earth. I put up my thumb and shut
one eye, and my thumb blotted out the planet Earth.
I didn't feel like a giant. I felt very, very small.

—Neil Armstrong

If we climb high enough, we will reach a height
from which tragedy ceases to look tragic.

—Irvin D. Yalom

The tragic or the humorous is a matter of perspective.

—Arnold Beisser

When you do find humor in trying times, one of the
first and most important changes you experience is
that you see your perplexing problems in a new way—
you suddenly have a new perspective on them.

—Allen Klein

You should never view your challenges as a disadvantage.
Instead, it's important for you to understand that
your experience facing and overcoming adversity
is actually one of your biggest advantages.

—Michelle Obama

When you're in the muck, you can only see muck. If
you somehow manage to float above it, you still see the
muck, but you see it from a different perspective.

—David Cronenberg

It isn't the things that happen to us in our lives that
cause us to suffer, it's how we relate to the things
that happen to us that causes us to suffer.

—Pema Chodron

Perspective is everything. How we look at a
circumstance determines our capacity for solving it.

—Stella Payton

We cling to our own point of view, as though everything
depended on it. Yet our opinions have no permanence;
like autumn and winter, they gradually pass away.

—Zhuangzi

Winners have the ability to step back from the canvas of
their lives like an artist gaining perspective. They make
their lives a work of art—an individual masterpiece.

—Denis Waitley

There is a huge amount of freedom that comes
to you when you take nothing personally.

—Don Miguel Ruiz

We can complain because rose bushes have
thorns, or rejoice because thorns have roses.

—Alphonse Karr

Loving people live in a loving world. Hostile
people live in a hostile world. Same world.

—Wayne Dyer

Every human life is made up of the light and the dark, the
happy and the sad, the vital and the deadening. How you
think about this rhythm of moods makes all the difference.

—Thomas Moore

There are seasons in life. Don't ever let anyone try to
deny you the joy of one season because they believe
you should stay in another season…. Listen to yourself.
Trust your instincts. Keep your perspective.

—Jane Clayson

It's not a bad lesson to learn in the bleaker months:
how you view a storm is a question of perspective;
provided you find the right rock to watch it from, it
could be the most incredible thing you'll ever witness.

—Dan Stevens

Most misunderstandings in the world could be
avoided if people would simply take the time
to ask, "What else could this mean?"

—Shannon L. Alder

Don't sweat the small stuff…and it's all small stuff.

—Richard Carlson (Attributed)

Seek Silence, Find Peace

Whenever I'm in a quandary about what to do about a situation or which direction to take in my life, I sit quietly, seek inner peace, and ask for guidance. What amazes me is that the right answer almost always comes along. It doesn't matter if it is a deep question about my life, a career related question, or even a relatively unimportant one, like which restaurant to go to that night; I trust the response. More often than not, in hindsight, it proves to be right one.

I think that the answers I get in silence are truer than those I'd get otherwise. It allows me to bypass the constant chatter of my mind, which often colors my answers with cloudiness. The stillness helps me to go right to the heart of the matter. It brings me peace of being, as well as peace of mind, because the answers come from a deeper, truer, place.

Silence could not only facilitate personal peace but, as a potential for bringing compassion and understanding for others, world peace as well.

In the midst of movement and chaos,
keep stillness inside of you.

—Deepak Chopra

Everything we do is infused with the energy in
which we do it. If we're frantic, life will be frantic.
If we are peaceful, life will be peaceful.

—Marianne Williamson

You do not need to leave your room. Remain sitting at your
table and listen. Do not even listen, simply wait, be quiet,
still, and solitary. The world will freely offer itself to you to be
unmasked, it has no choice, it will roll in ecstasy at your feet.

—Franz Kafka

Within us resides a special sanctuary: our inner
temple of peace, harmony, and inner reflection.
It's just a matter of tapping into it.

—Ros Ben-Moshe

Peace comes from within.

—The Buddha

We can never obtain peace in the outer world
until we make peace with ourselves.

—Dalai Lama

If there's no inner peace, people can't give it to you.
The husband can't give it to you. Your children
can't give it to you. You have to give it to you.

—Linda Evans

Never be in a hurry; do everything quietly and in a
calm spirit. Do not lose your inner peace for anything
whatsoever, even if your whole world seems upset.

—Saint Francis de Sales

If in our daily life we can smile, if we can be peaceful
and happy, not only we, but everyone will profit from
it. This is the most basic kind of peace work.

—Thich Nhat Hanh

Peace begins with a smile.

—Mother Teresa

You find peace not by rearranging the circumstances of
your life, but by realizing who you are at the deepest level.

—Eckhart Tolle

We don't realize that, somewhere within us all,
there does exist a supreme self who is eternally at peace.

—Elizabeth Gilbert

Peacefulness is not the absence of external difficulties or
conflict. Instead, it is an internal relationship to whatever
is happening, whether it is pleasant, painful, or neutral.

—Noah Levine

Peace is the result of retraining your mind to process
life as it is, rather than as you think it should be.

—Wayne Dyer

The first step in becoming a more peaceful person
is to have the humility to admit that, in most cases,
you're creating your own emergencies. Life will
usually go on if things don't go according to plan.

—Richard Carlson

Do not let the behavior of others destroy your inner peace.

—Dalai Lama

When everything is moving and shifting, the only
way to counteract chaos is stillness. When things
feel extraordinary, strive for ordinary. When the
surface is wavy, dive deeper for quieter waters.

—Kristin Armstrong

You can't solve chaos with more chaos.

—Erin Gilmore

Seek out a tree and let it teach you stillness.

—Eckhart Tolle

Little things seem nothing, but they give peace, like
those meadow flowers which individually seem
odorless, but all together perfume the air.

—Georges Bernanos

There's nothing like the peace of the countryside, the quiet
and the lack of distraction.
It helps you to focus your mind.

—Jenny Nimmo

I see the world being slowly transformed into a wilderness;
I hear the approaching thunder that, one day, will destroy
us too. I feel the suffering of millions. And yet, when I
look up at the sky, I somehow feel that everything will
change for the better, that this cruelty too shall end,
that peace and tranquility will return once more.

—Anne Frank

We shall find peace. We shall hear angels,
we shall see the sky sparkling with diamonds.

—Anton Chekhov

If everyone demanded peace instead of another
television set, then there'd be peace.

—John Lennon

Peace and love are just as contagious as anger and
fear. Your mindset affects the people around you
and perpetually changes the world. The question
is—what kind of world are you creating? What
new society are you thinking into existence?

—Vironika Tugaleva

Peace is not a relationship of nations. It is a condition
of mind brought about by a serenity of soul. Peace is
not merely the absence of war. It is also a state of mind.
Lasting peace can come only to peaceful people.

—Jawaharlal Nehru

It isn't enough to talk about peace. One must believe in it.
And it isn't enough to believe in it. One must work at it.

—Eleanor Roosevelt

Peace is a daily, a weekly, a monthly process,
gradually changing opinions, slowly eroding old
barriers, quietly building new structures.

—John F. Kennedy

Even a little peace, a little love, a little forgiveness,
and a little kindness can change the world for the
better and bring it closer to universal peace.

—Debasish Mridha

Did I offer peace today? Did I bring a smile to someone's face? Did I say words of healing? Did I let go of my anger and resentment? Did I forgive? Did I love? These are the real questions. I must trust that the little bit of love that I sow now will bear many fruits, here in this world and the life to come.

—Henri Nouwen

Every day we could think about the aggression in the world… everybody always strikes out at the enemy, and the pain escalates forever. Every day we could reflect on this and ask ourselves, "Am I going to add to the aggression in the world? …Am I going to practice peace, or am I going to war?"

—Pema Chodron

While you are proclaiming peace with your lips, be careful to have it even more fully in your heart.

—Saint Francis of Assisi

When the crowded Vietnamese refugee boats met with storms or pirates, if everyone panicked, all would be lost. But if even one person on the boat remained calm and centered, it was enough. It showed the way for everyone to survive.

—Thich Nhat Hanh

Seize the Day

Many years ago, my husband and I visited Chiang Mai, Thailand. On the first evening there, we headed out of our hotel to go to dinner at a restaurant recommended in our guidebook. In the lobby, we passed a flier announcing a local street food festival that evening. We hesitated to go there, not knowing what the food would be like and how safe it might be to eat. But we seized the moment and went anyway. And we were glad we did.

The evening was incredible. The busy and beautifully decorated streets were lined with numerous food booths. We could not identify most of what was being cooked, but it all emitted mouth-watering smells. There were also demonstrations of food-carving, with people making such things as an elephant out of a watermelon, as well as other Thai craft items.

The highlight for us was not only the food and the visual delights but also the kindness of the people. We ordered a delicious Thai chicken stew at one of the booths, but there was no place to sit and eat it. All the tables and chairs in the street were taken. When the merchant who'd served us the chicken stew saw that, he and his wife got up from behind the counter, brought the chairs on which they had been sitting to a table, and invited us to sit down and enjoy our meal.

I'm sure the restaurant in the guidebook would have been decent, but probably not as special or as memorable as our spur-of-the-moment seize-the-day experience.

Life is full of beauty. Notice it. Notice the bumble bee, the small child, and the smiling faces. Smell the rain and feel the wind. Live your life to the fullest potential, and fight for your dreams.

—Ashley Smith

Don't wait for extraordinary opportunities. Seize common occasions and make them great.

—Orison S. Marden

Seize the moment. Remember all those women on the *Titanic* who waved off the dessert cart.

—Erma Bombeck

Don't tell me that the sky's the limit when there are footprints on the moon.

—Paul Brandt

Do not follow where the path may lead. Go instead
where there is no path and leave a trail.

—Ralph Waldo Emerson

Life begins at the end of your comfort zone.

—Neale Donald Walsch

Go for it now. The future is promised to no one.

—Wayne Dyer

Every day one should at least hear one little song,
read one good poem, see one fine painting, and—
if at all possible—speak a few sensible words.

—Johann Wolfgang von Goethe

If you're alive, you've got to flap your arms and legs, you've got to jump around a lot, you've got to make a lot of noise, because life is the very opposite of death. And therefore, as I see it, if you're quiet, you're not living. You've got to be noisy, or at least your thoughts should be noisy, colorful, and lively.

—Mel Brooks

Why not upset the apple cart? If you don't, the apples will rot anyway.

—Frank A. Clark

Every day we are engaged in a miracle which we don't even recognize: a blue sky, white clouds, green leaves, the black curious eyes of a child—our own two eyes. All is a miracle.

—Thich Nhat Hanh

To live is so startling it leaves little time for anything else.

—Emily Dickinson

Don't settle. Don't finish crappy books. If you
don't like the menu, leave the restaurant. If
you're not on the right path, get off it.

—Chris Brogan

Incredible change happens in your life when you
decide to take control of what you do have power over
instead of craving control over what you don't.

—Steve Maraboli

Only I can change my life. No one can do it for me.

—Carol Burnett

The most common way people give up their
power is by thinking they don't have any.

—Alice Walker

No one is in control of your happiness but you;
therefore, you have the power to change anything
about yourself or your life that you want to change.

—Barbara de Angelis

Each person holds so much power within themselves
that needs to be let out. Sometimes they just need a
little nudge, a little direction, a little support, a little
coaching, and the greatest things can happen.

—Pete Carroll

People are always blaming their circumstances for
what they are. I don't believe in circumstances.
The people who get on in this world are the people
who get up and look for the circumstances they
want, and, if they can't find them, make them.

—George Bernard Shaw

The only limits in one's life are self-imposed.

—Denis Waitley

Some days there won't be a song in your heart. Sing anyway.

—Emory Austin

Make everything that happens to you meaningful.
If you're stuck in traffic, instead of fuming, try
putting a blessing on everyone around you.

—Brian Browne Walker

You never let a serious crisis go to waste. And
what I mean by that is it's an opportunity to do
things you thought you could not do before.

—Rahm Emanuel

When written in Chinese, the word "crisis" is
composed of two characters. One represents
danger and the other represents opportunity.

—John F. Kennedy

Behold the tortoise. He makes progress
only when he sticks his neck out.

—James B. Conant

Living at risk is jumping off the cliff and
building your wings on the way down.

—Ray Bradbury

When you're skating on thin ice, you may as well tap-dance.

—Bryce Courtenay

Every day brings a chance for you to draw in a
breath, kick off your shoes, and dance.

—Oprah Winfrey

I love life. I think it's fantastic. Sometimes it deals hard
things, and when it deals great things, you have to seize them.

—Sam Taylor-Wood

Don't judge each day by the harvest you
reap but by the seeds that you plant.

—Robert Louis Stevenson

Learn from nature. Stuff lives and stuff dies all the time,
you know: animals and birds and flowers. Trees come and
go, and we come and go. That's it. So we should all seize
life and make the most of what we have while we can.

—Joanna Lumley

First I was dying to finish high school and start college.
And then I was dying to finish college and start working.
And then I was dying to marry and have children.
And then I was dying for my children to grow old enough so
I could return to work.
And then I was dying to retire.
And now I am dying—
and suddenly I realize I forgot to live.

—Anonymous

Yesterday is gone. Tomorrow has not yet come. We have only today. Let us begin.

—Mother Teresa

Take Courage

I suspect that the word "courage" has different meanings for different people. For one person, it might take a great deal of courage just to get out of bed in the morning after dealing with the loss of a loved one. For a firefighter, it might be having the courage to run into a burning building to save a pet. Or for others, it might be as simple as getting up enough courage to ask for help when they are not doing well. For me, it was when I was asked to lead a weekend on therapeutic humor for a burn survivors retreat.

As I wrote in a previous book, *You Can't Ruin My Day*:

> When I was first asked to do the retreat, I didn't know how I could possibly teach this group of people to laugh when they had been through such a horrific ordeal. I didn't know how I would react to their disfigurement. I didn't know how I could sustain such a long period of time with them. Would I have enough material to fill the weekend? Would it be relevant to them? After all, they had been through hell. I hadn't.

> The truth was that all my fears were unfounded. They loved what I did. They jumped at any chance to laugh. And once I got over the initial shock of seeing their deformities, all I could see was their radiant and beautiful spirit. They didn't know it, but they taught me more than I taught them....

They taught me about unconditional love as I watched their caretakers and loved ones attend to the burn survivors' every need.

They taught me that despite what they went through, they could laugh. In fact, they craved it.

They taught me how to face the unknown with grace and determination and how to get on with life in spite of circumstances. But most of all, they taught me about courage.

I almost turned this engagement down. But I'm so glad I didn't. I will never forget these brave and courageous souls.

Courage takes many forms. There is physical courage, there is moral courage. Then there is a still higher type of courage—the courage to brave pain, to live with it, to never let others know of it, and to still find joy in life; to wake up in the morning with an enthusiasm for the day ahead.

—Howard Cosell

Anyone can slay a dragon…but try waking up every morning and loving the world all over again. That's what takes a real hero.

—Brian Andreas

To face despair and not give in to it, that's courage.

—Ted Koppel

The greatest test of courage is to bear defeat without losing heart.

—Robert G. Ingersoll

To be courageous means to be afraid but
to go a little step forward anyway.

—Beverly Smith

Success is not final, failure is not fatal:
it is the courage to continue that counts.

—Winston Churchill

Courage is not having the strength to go on;
it is going on when you don't have the strength.

—Theodore Roosevelt

Strength is granted to us all when we are
needed to serve great causes.

—Winston Churchill

When everything seems to be going against you, remember
that the airplane takes off against the wind, not with it.

—Henry Ford

Grant me the courage not to give up even
though I think it is hopeless.

—Chester W. Nimitz

God, grant me the serenity to accept the things
I cannot change, courage to change the things I
can, and wisdom to know the difference.

—Reinhold Niebuhr

You gain strength, courage, and confidence by every
experience in which you really stop to look fear in the
face. You are able to say to yourself, "I lived through this
horror. I can take the next thing that comes along."

—Eleanor Roosevelt

Courage is resistance to fear, mastery
of fear—not absence of fear.

—Mark Twain

The only thing we have to fear is fear itself.

—Franklin D. Roosevelt

Feel the fear, and do it anyway

—Susan Jeffers

The only courage that matters is the kind that gets you from one moment to the next.

—Mignon Mclaughlin

Don't be afraid to take a big step if one is indicated. You can't cross a chasm in two small jumps.

—David Lloyd George

I learned that courage was not the absence of fear, but the triumph over it. The brave man is not he who does not feel afraid, but he who conquers that fear.

—Nelson Mandela

You can't be brave if you've only had
wonderful things happen to you.

—Mary Tyler Moore

Difficulties are meant to rouse, not discourage.
The human spirit is to grow strong by conflict.

—William Ellery Channing

Adversity causes some men to break; others to break records.

—William Arthur Ward

I would never have amounted to anything were it not
for adversity. I was forced to come up the hard way.

—J. C. Penney

The difficulties, hardships, and trials of life, the
obstacles…are positive blessings. They knit the
muscles more firmly, and teach self-reliance.

—William Matthew

No tree becomes rooted and sturdy unless many a wind assails it. For by its very tossing it tightens its grip and plants its roots more securely; the fragile trees are those that have grown in a sunny valley.

—Seneca

Nobody is born with courage. You have to develop courage the same way you do a muscle.

—Maya Angelou

Life shrinks or expands in proportion to one's courage.

—Anaïs Nin

Courage is contagious. When a brave man takes a stand, the spines of others are often stiffened.

—Billy Graham

Life is a series of experiences, each one of which makes us bigger, even though sometimes it is hard to realize this.

—Henry Ford

Nothing splendid has ever been achieved except
by those who dared believe that something
inside them was superior to circumstance.

—Bruce Barton

What does not destroy me, makes me strong.

—Friedrich Nietzsche

Should you shield the canyons from the windstorms,
you would never see the beauty of their carvings.

—Elisabeth Kübler-Ross

Through each crisis in my life, with acceptance
and hope, in a single defining moment, I finally
gained the courage to do things differently.

—Sharon E. Rainey

If all our misfortunes were laid in one common heap
whence everyone must take an equal portion, most people
would be contented to take their own and depart.

—Socrates

Something I learned along the way is that you really have
to have courage in life. You can do amazing things on
any level. It doesn't have to change the world; it can just
impact the people around you—that's just as amazing.

—Joy Mangano

All our dreams can come true—if you we
have the courage to pursue them.

—Walt Disney

Shoot for the moon. Even if you miss it,
you will land among the stars.

—Les Brown

I think laughter may be a form of courage. As humans, we sometimes stand tall and look into the sun and laugh, and I think we are never more brave than when we do that.

—Linda Ellerbee

Courage is not the towering oak that sees storms come and go; it is the fragile blossom that opens in the snow.

—Alice M. Swaim

Courage doesn't always roar. Sometimes courage is the little voice at the end of the day that says, "I'll try again tomorrow."

—Mary Anne Radmacher

Trust Your Higher Power

I was born and raised in New York City. For the past forty-years, or so, I've lived in San Francisco, but I visit my hometown at least once a year.

In the past, I used to stay with my cousin who lived in Queens, but she passed away. So since then, I've either rented an apartment from an acquaintance who has a time-share, or from a friend who lives in Connecticut but has an apartment in Manhattan. One particular year, the first apartment wasn't available, and my friend had just sold his place. I had no place to stay.

Then, one day, I accompanied my husband, who is a therapist, to his annual conference dinner in San Francisco. During the cocktail hour, a woman came over to us, looked me straight in the eye and said, "You are so debonair. You are so cute. You are…." I did have a jacket and nice tie on, but nothing, I thought, likely to attract such glowing compliments.

Since people were attending the conference from all over the world, I asked her where she was from. She said, "New York City."

"We will be going there in a few months," I said. "Do you know of any apartments we could rent?" She wanted to know when we would be there. I told her the last week in May.

She said, and this is the incredible part, "We will be in Italy that week. You can stay at our apartment." When I asked what she would charge us, she said "Nothing. We just like someone to watch the apartment when we are gone."

I have had many of these "mini-miracles" happen throughout my life. In the past, I've often questioned how such amazing things could happen. After all, I had never met this woman, I didn't even know she was at the cocktail hour or that she lived in New York City. Yet she was drawn to me and happened to be going to Europe at exactly the same time we needed a place to stay in her city.

Those mini-miracles still astound me, but the more they happen, the more I realize the presence of a higher power within my life.

I'm not a religious person by any means. But I certainly believe in some kind of a higher power and something looking out for me. I've definitely had angels that have either guided me or helped me through moments in my life, without a doubt.

—Christian Slater

When you trust your inner guidance and begin moving in the direction of your dreams…you will be cloaked in an armor bestowed upon you by your guardian angel.

—Charles F. Glassman

We all have angels guiding us. They look after us. They heal us, touch us, and comfort us with invisible warm hands. What will bring their help? Asking. Giving thanks.

—Sophy Burnham

If I'm cradling a question in my heart, to be shown the
right direction, I pay intense attention to the answers
that come, no matter what delivery service God may use.
License plates, billboards, songs on the radio, comments
from strangers, all become grist for my own spiritual mill.

—Tosha Silver

When we recognize the Divine Presence everywhere,
then we know that it responds to us and that there is a
Law of God, a Law of Love, forever giving of itself to us.

—Ernest Holmes

When you focus on the journey, you will be blessed
with guardian angels to direct your path.

—Lailah Gifty Akita

I truly believe that everything that we do and everyone that we meet is put in our path for a purpose. There are no accidents; we're all teachers—if we're willing to pay attention to the lessons we learn, trust our positive instincts, and not be afraid to take risks or wait for some miracle to come knocking at our door.

—Marla Gibbs

What the universe will manifest when you are in alignment with it is a lot more interesting than what you try to manifest.

—Adyashanti

When we stop trying to control events, they fall into a natural order, an order that works. We're at rest while a power much greater than our own takes over, and it does a much better job than we could have done. We learn to trust that the power that holds galaxies together can handle the circumstances of our relatively little lives.

—Marianne Williamson

It's important to have a vision of the long run and make wise decisions for our highest good in the present moment; however, we don't want to become attached to how everything must look. When we show up in good faith, life provides. And when we trust, we are always in the flow of manifestation.

—Alaric Hutchinson

I have unshakeable faith in the perfect outcome of every situation in my life, for I am allowing God to be in absolute control and guide me in all proper actions.

—Catherine Ponder

I have faith that all is well, that all good things come to me in divine timing. I can relax and surrender to the truth that I am divinely guided and cared for.

—Eileen Anglin

The best way to handle life is to put your life in God's hands.

—Anthony Liccione

If you anchor yourself in Divine Source, what needs
to come will always come, regardless of others.

—Tosha Silver

Know that you are divinely guided and watched
over in every moment of every day.

—Eileen Anglin

The most glorious moment you will ever experience
in your life is when you look back and see how
God was protecting you all this time.

—Shannon L. Alder

I love God, and when you get to know Him,
you find He's a Livin' Doll.

—Jane Russell

You're worthy because the Great Spirit, or Universe, or God, or whatever you want to call a higher power, has put you on the earth at this time. There's nothing else to think about! Since you're as worthy as the next person, you're as deserving to receive as anyone else. Anything else that your mind says around that is made-up, non-supportive crapola!

—T. Harv Eker

In the middle of what seem like our darkest, craziest patterns is a ground of basic sanity and basic goodness that is untarnished and indestructible.

—Geneen Roth

A wisdom as constant as the North Star shines within all of us. It is always present. waiting to be tapped, waiting to guide us, to advise us…. No matter what our background, profession, color, or religion, employing this universal compass, this innate sense of what we know to be true, will help us establish a lifelong foundation—a place we go to recover our sanity and to regain our balance.

—Nancy Cobb

There is no greater gift than realizing the
constant presence of the Divine and His Absolute
Power to create and restore all things.

—Marta Mrotek

When things go wrong, we have one of two
choices to make. We can choose to respond with
fear, or we can choose to respond with faith.

—Penny Hunt

When God requires us to surrender one dream,
it's because He wants to hand us a bigger and better one.

—Mandy Hale

You start to live when you commit your life to a cause
higher than yourself. You must learn to depend on
divine power for the fulfillment of a higher calling.

—Lailah Gifty Akita

There is trust in there being a Spirit who loves me and wants
me to have love in my life. I trust in this higher power, it is
what keeps me moving forward no matter what happens.

—Kenny Loggins

Do little things in an extraordinary way. You
must not let your life run in the ordinary way;
do something that will dazzle the world. Show
that God's creative principle works in you.

—Paramahansa Yogananda

There is no situation that could ever confront you that
cannot be solved. Life takes on real meaning when you set
values for yourself, regard yourself as worthwhile, and elevate
your thoughts to things that are of God-good. There is a
higher power. Turn to it and use it; it is yours for the asking.

—Bryan Adams

Closing Thought

In 2014, I traveled to Israel to attend a wedding. Since the bride's mother was Moroccan, a traditional henna ceremony was performed. Relatives gathered, painted their hands with henna, and danced to traditional Moroccan music while carrying trays of cookies. Both the men and the women wore gold-embroidered costumes; the men also donned fez hats.

Suddenly, during the ceremony, sirens blasted loudly in the small town where we were staying. I thought about running to the cement bomb shelter, which nearly every house in Israel had, but being a visitor from another country, I waited to see what others would do.

Surprisingly, nobody moved. They were all stunned, since they were unaccustomed to sirens going off in the area. It had been over twenty years since they had last heard them.

The sirens and missile attacks continued for several days. It reminded me of growing up in New York City during World War II. My dad was an air raid warden who rushed out of the house to do his job every time the sirens sounded. It was very frightening for me at five years old, especially since this usually occurred in the middle of the night.

In Israel, those sirens triggered the same fears. I tried to logically calm myself down, but nothing worked until I remembered the words written by James Dillet Freeman in his Prayer for Protection. It was repeating those simple words over and over again that helped me to overcome my traumatic situation.

Words can be more powerful than you realize. It is why I share the positive ones in this book. And why I leave you with the prayer I used to ease that troubling time in my life:

> The light of God surrounds me;
> The love of God enfolds me;
> The power of God protects me;
> The presence of God watches over me.
> Wherever I am, God is!

Index

About the Author

Allen Klein is an award-winning professional keynote speaker and best-selling author. He is a recipient of a Lifetime Achievement Award from the Association for Applied and Therapeutic Humor, a Certified Speaking Professional designation from the National Speakers Association, and a Communication and Leadership Award from Toastmasters International, and he is an inductee in the Hunter College, New York City, Hall of Fame.

Klein is also the author of twenty-six books including *The Healing Power of Humor, Embracing Life After Loss, The Courage to Laugh, Change Your Life!: A Little Book of Big Ideas, Secrets Kids Know*, and *You Can't Ruin My Day*. In addition, he is also a TEDx presenter on the power of intention. (http://tinyurl.com/z4hfsx5)

For more information about Klein's books or presentations, go to www.allenklein.com or contact him at: allen@allenklein.com.